THE SHOW-STOPPER

Written and Illustrated
by
Joanna Greenwood

ISBN: 9781980241522

With Best Wishes,

Jo Greenwood

> Guidance Notes can be found at the back of this book,
> to enable use of the story to help with
> exploration and development of
> behaviour and social skills.

Also available in the **Yew Tree Woodland Tales** series-

Book 1- New Kid on the Block by Joanna Greenwood
ISBN 9781549821547

For Dad, Noo, Grandad and Gran-
With all of whom I'd love to share this book.

Each night in woods
near Yew Tree Farm,
when all was still
and dark and calm,

Mole loved to dig deep in the ground
and pile the earth into great mounds ...

Then every molehill he would start
to sculpt into the finest art!

You see, as Mole had such a flare,
and took the most painstaking care,
the animals he did create
looked so much like his own best mates!

For ages the
mole's secret skill
lay hid, as just
wee sculptures, 'til ...

One night he built with love and stealth
a life-size model of himself!

As Mouse passed by,
just the next day,
he asked 'Mole' if
he'd like to play?

Confused when 'Mole' did not react
(the sculpture's detail so exact),

Mouse guessed at last and found it funny,
that this friend here was just a dummy!

The work involved Mole didn't mind,
as Mouse's offer was so kind.

He started building straight away,
and had all finished by Show Day ...

"... or so he thought, but while he slept,
on Show Day eve, a creature crept ...

The nosy fox was also sly–
he couldn't wait, so came to spy
on Mole's display of perfect art,
but felt a *pang* within his heart ...

He wished he too could be as good
at crafting, in this neighbourhood!

With anger then he **HIT** the 'Owl'–
an act of malice, mean and foul ...

For then another
passed by there.
Goat marvelled
at art everywhere ...

On his way home, this was a treat
built to standards hard to beat-
Though one statue did not look right,
and Mole had turned-in for the night!

Goat chewed some soil,
and patted it,
to make the head
a perfect fit.

Thrilled with his fix
he danced about,
delighted that
he'd helped Mole out ...

Mole wondered, of his friends, who could
have caused such damage in their wood?

Right at this point, drawn by the sound,
more creatures came and gathered round ...

Including a now timid one–
Fox was ashamed of what he'd done!

On hearing Mole tell all their friends
how Goat needed to make amends,
his heart began to feel real bad
at seeing Goat feeling so sad.

The fox agreed. To put it right,
he vowed to work all through the night.
Preparing soil to act as glue,
between each broken piece he flew ...

MOLE'S
ART
SHOW
NOON
TODAY!

The animals went back to bed,
leaving Fox to sort his head!

Nearing noon, Owl spoke again-

With Mole's teaching,
each learned a skill,
and helped him mend the art until ...

A wonderful display stood there-
all made with love,
friendship and care.

Information for Parents, Carers and Teachers

This story is aimed as a discussion tool to help children explore 'right and wrong' behaviour choices.

It poses a moral dilemma as to 'who is to blame?' for stopping Mole's show, whilst still encouraging children to understand the concepts of 'putting things right again' after mistakes are made, and teamwork.

Who was the naughtiest- Fox or Goat? There is no definitive answer to this problem, as the characters have both made mistakes, although it is hoped that the tale will allow plenty of debate.

Some children may think the outcome of their actions and likely punishment is the most important factor (ie. Goat broke the most statues).

Others may agree with Owl- that intention is key (ie. Goat had the best intentions, despite the consequences).

The story is loosely based on moral reasoning theories (such as those of Jean Piaget and Lawrence Kohlberg) that explain that our reasoning skills develop in stages- from showing more self-driven, outcome-based reactions, when we are little; to more complex decision-making as we age, involving other factors such as peer-pressure and agreed rule-changing.

Therefore, there may be a trend from young children largely blaming Goat (the greatest destruction) towards older children feeling Fox was the worst (for intentionally destroying a statue).

As all children develop at different rates though, there may be a mixture of viewpoints on the story, which hopes to give some insight as to how each individual reader judges moral situations, and whether they yet recognise feelings such as guilt, blame, regret, social pressures, consequence of own actions and empathy for others.

Suggested Discussion Questions

The following questions are merely suggestions for discussion, as there will no doubt be a wide range of individual viewpoints on the story events, beyond those answers given here (depending on which character's behaviour and emotions the individual reader can identify with). Conversation around the questions may help children to see alternative behaviour choices and/or feelings of their own or others, in similar situations.

How did Mole feel when he was asked to put on a show? Surprised, proud, happy, nervous, special...

What did Fox feel when he saw the display? Jealous, angry, frustrated, nosy...

How did he feel after he'd knocked the head off the 'Owl' statue? Happy, worried, sorry, scared, didn't care.

Why did Fox run away afterwards? He was scared he would get into trouble, or he didn't care.

Did Fox do the 'right' thing in running away afterwards?   What else could he have done?
- He could have stayed and explained to Mole what he'd done.
- Or he could have tried to repair the statue, or woken Mole and offered to repair it.

Did Goat do the 'right' thing in trying to repair the statue?   What else could he have done?
- He did do the 'right' thing as he tried to help Mole by fixing it.
- Or, he could have asked Mole first if he needed help; or waited until morning to ask his permission.
- Or he could have tried to find out who had broken the statue, and asked them to repair it.

Why did Goat hide afterwards? He was scared he would get into trouble, ashamed he'd ruined everything...

How did Mole feel when he saw the broken display? Angry, upset, sad, shocked, confused, disappointed...

How did Mole feel about Goat and Fox, once they had BOTH explained that they'd caused the damage?
- Shocked, annoyed, angry, confused, hurt, not sure who to blame...
- He may have understood Goat's reasons more.

Who do you think had been the 'naughtiest'- Fox or Goat?   Why?
a) FOX because-
   - He was jealous and broke a statue on purpose; whereas Goat had only tried to help Mole out.
   - He ran away afterwards.
   - He let Goat take the blame, at first.
   - If he hadn't broken the 'Owl' statue, Goat wouldn't have needed to try repairing it in the first place.

b) GOAT because-
   - He broke more/all of the statues.
   - He interfered with (and damaged) the display without asking Mole first.
   - He was silly dancing around after fixing the statue, as that caused it to fall over and break everything.

How did Fox and Goat both feel after they had been told off? Upset, sorry, embarrassed, ashamed...

How did both animals eventually try to make things better again?   Did it work?
- Goat and Fox both said sorry to Mole, and tried to repair the damage they'd caused.
- It was too hard for them to fix on their own in time.

How did Owl help sort out the problem?
- He pointed out that Goat and Fox had both made mistakes they had now learned from, and saw that both
  were really sorry.
- He suggested that all the animals help repair the mess in time for the show, to support Mole.

24127062R00021

Printed in Poland
by Amazon Fulfillment
Poland Sp. z o.o., Wrocław